Alpern's Architectural Aphorisms

a commodious compendium of convenient quotations

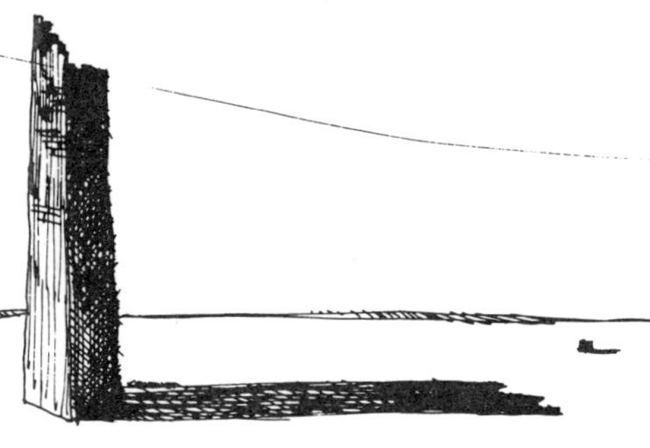

Andrew Alpern, AIA

Library of Congress Catalog Card Number 79-91127

Alpern's
Architectural
Aphorisms
a commodious
compendium of
convenient quotations
compiled by
Andrew Alpern, AIA
illustrated by
Peter Kraemer
an Architectural Record book
AR

ON ARCHITECTS

The fate of the architect is the strangest of all. How often he expends his whole soul, his whole heart and passion, to produce buildings into which he himself may never enter.

~Goethe: *Elective Affinities*, Book II, Ch. 3

A lawyer, without history or literature, is a mechanic. A mere working mason, if he possesses some knowledge of these, he may venture to call himself an architect.

~Sir Walter Scott: *Guy Mannering*, Ch. 37

HERE
IS
THE

ON PROFESSIONAL RESPONSIBILITY

When thou buildest a new house, then thou shalt make a parapet for thy roof, that thou shalt not bring blood upon thy house, if any man fall from thence.

~Deuteronomy 22:8

If a builder build a house for a man and do not make its construction firm and the house which he has built collapse and cause the death of the owner of the house .... that builder shall be put to death.

If it cause the death of the son of the owner of the house .... they shall put to death the son of that builder.

If it cause the death of a slave of the owner of the house .... he shall give to the owner of the house a slave of equal value.

If it destroy property, he shall restore what ever it destroyed, and because he did not make the house which he built firm and it collapsed he shall rebuild the house which collapsed at his own expense. If a builder build a house for a man and do not make its construction meet the requirements, and a wall fall in, that builder shall strengthen the wall at his own expense.

~Hammurabi: *Code of Laws* (2200 B.C.)

Woe unto him that buildeth his house by unrighteousness, and his chambers by wrong; that useth his neighbors service without wages, and giveth him not for his work.

~Jeremiah 22:13

ON NOT RETAINING A PROFESSIONAL

That far land we dream about
Where every man is his own architect.
~Robert Browning: *Red Cotton Nightcap Country*, Pt. II

And they shall build houses, and inhabit them;
And they shall plant vineyards, and eat the fruit of them.
They shall not build, and another inhabit;
They shall not plant, and another eat.
--Isaiah 65: 22

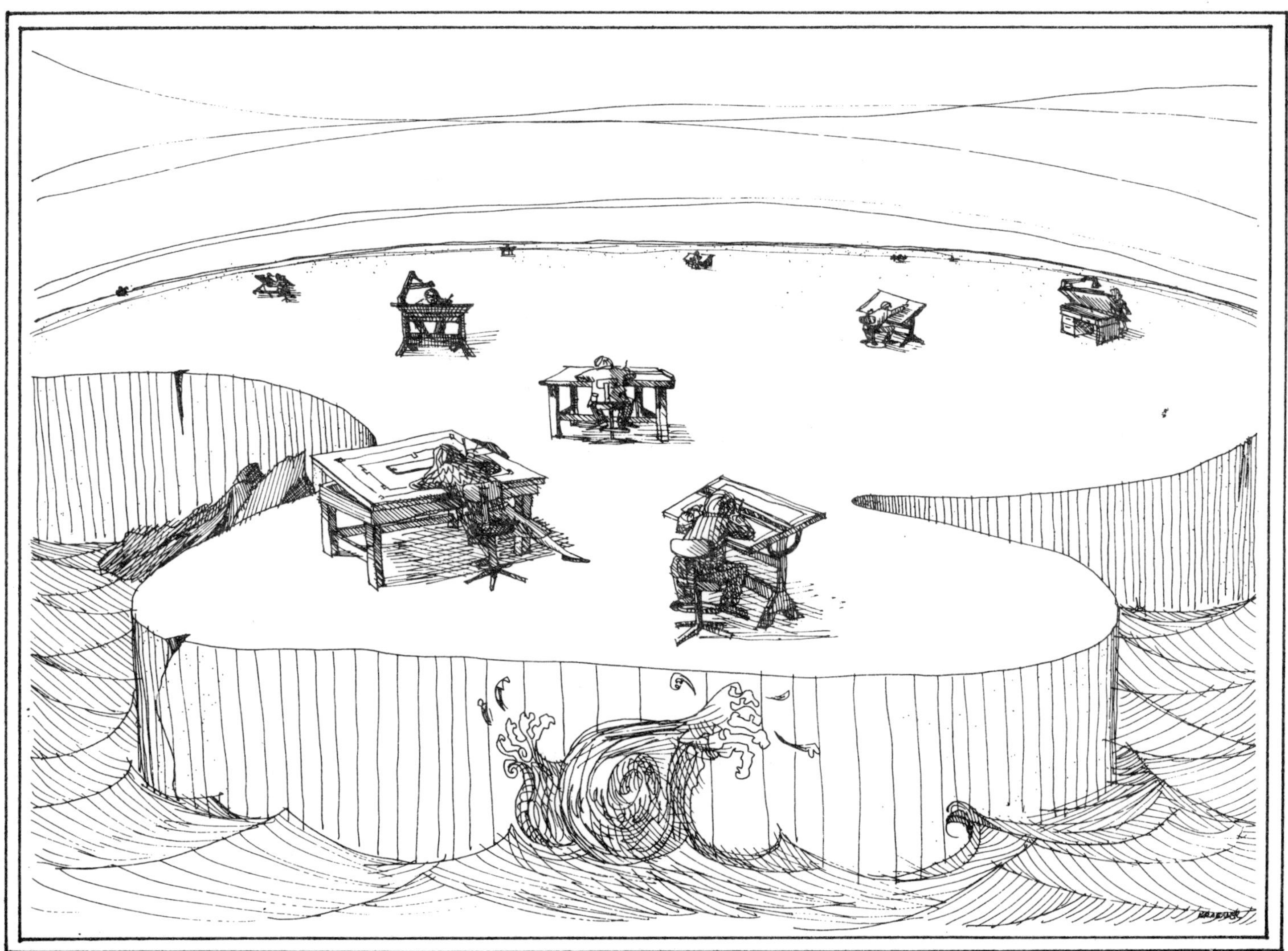

ON BUILDING

If I build a church, though I do not really want one, let it be in the wilderness, out of nothing but nail-holes.

~ Stanley Kunitz : *Revolving Meditation*

And they said, go to, Let us build a city and a tower, whose top may reach unto heaven.

~Genesis 12:4

ON BUILDERS VS. ARCHITECTS

The whole difference between construction and creation is exactly this: that a thing constructed can only be loved after it is constructed; but a thing created is loved before it exists.

~G.K Chesterton; *Preface to Dicken's Pickwick Papers*

A man that has a taste of music, painting, or architecture, is like one that has another sense, when compared with such as have no relish of these arts.

~Joseph Addison: *The Spectator*, No. 93 (1711)

ON ARCHITECTURE

Architecture, sculpture, painting, music and poetry, may truly be called the efflorescence of civilized life.

~Herbert Spencer: *Essays on Education* (1861)

I call architecture frozen music.

~Goethe: *Letter to Eckermann* (1829)

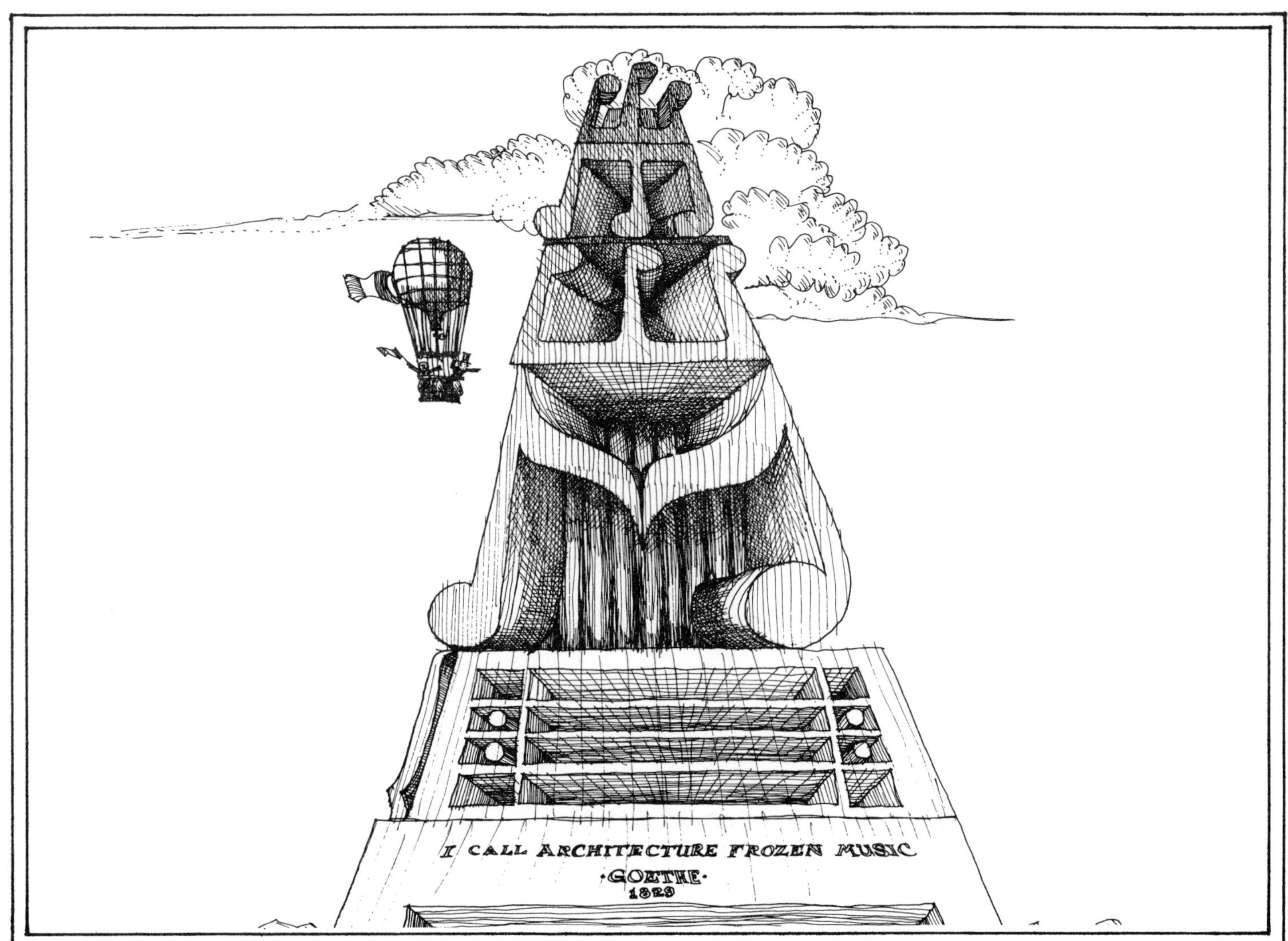
I CALL ARCHITECTURE FROZEN MUSIC
·GOETHE·
1829

The art of dancing stands at the source of all the arts that express themselves first in the human person. The art of building, or architecture, is the begining of all the arts that lie out side the person; and in the end they unite.

—Havelock Ellis: *The Dance of Life* (1923)

I must study politics and war, that my sons may have liberty to study mathematics and philosophy, geography, natural history and naval architecture, navigation, commerce, and agriculture, in order to give their children a right to study painting, poetry, music, architecture, statuary, tapestry, and porcelain.

~John Adams: *Letter to his Wife* (1780)

We shape our buildings and then our buildings shape us.

~Winston Churchill

ON REAL ESTATE:

Every man has by nature the right to possess property as his own.

~Pope Leo XIII *Rerum Novarum* (1891)

Every man holds his property subject to the general right of the community to regulate its use to whatever degree the public welfare may require it.

~Theodore Roosevelt: *Speach at Osawatomie* (1910)

Broad acres are a patent of nobility; and no man but feels more of a man in the word if he have a bit of ground that he can call his own. However small it is on the surface, it is four thousand miles deep; and that is a very handsome property.

~ Charles Dudly Warner (1829–1900): *My Summer in a Garden*

Property has its duties as well as its rights.

~Disraeli: *Sybil* (1845)

Buy land. They aren't making it anymore.

~Mark Twain.

Few rich people own their property. The property owns them.

~Robert Green Ingersoll; *Address to The McKinley League* (1896)

Property is theft.

~Pierre Joseph Proudhon (1809-1865)

NOT
FOR
SALE

ON DESIGN PLANNING

These unhappy times call for the building of plans......
that build from the bottom up and not from the
top down.

~Franklin Delano Roosevelt : *Radio Address* (1932)

That saith, I will build me a wide house and
large chambers, and cutteth him out windows;
and — it is roofed with cedar and painted with
vermilion.

~Jeremiah 22:14

And there were windows in three rows and light was against light in three ranks. And all the doors and posts were square with the windows.

~ I Kings 7:4-5

Moreover Uzziah built towers in Jerusalem at the corner gate, and at the valley gate, and at the turning of the wall, and fortified them.

~ II Chronicles 26:9

He couldn't design a cathedral without it looking like the First Supernatural Bank.

~Eugene O'Neill : *The Great God Brown*

Three things are to be looked to in a building: that it stand in the right spot; that it be securely founded; that it be successfully executed.

~Goethe : *Elective Affinities, Book I, Ch. 9*

The youth gets together his materials to build
a bridge to the moon, or, perchance, a palace or temple
on earth, and, at length, the middle-aged man
concludes to build a woodshed with them.

~Henry David Thoreau: *Journal* (1852)

Better build schoolrooms for the Boy
Then cells and gibbets for The Man

~ ~Eliza Cook (1818~1889): *Song for the Ragged Schools*

ON CITY PLANNING

Let the street be as wide as the height of the houses.

~Leonardo da Vinci, *Notebooks*

ON URBAN RENEWAL

And he said, this will I do; I will pull down my barns and build greater.

~St. Luke 12:18

ON HISTORIC PRESERVATION

Thou shalt not remove thy neighbor's landmark, which they of old time have set in thine inheritance.

~Deuteronomy 27:17

ON MEETING BUCKMINSTER FULLER

Shut thee from heaven with a dome more vast, till thou at length art free.

~Oliver Wendell Holmes; *The Autocrat of the Breakfast Table*.

ON LAND SURVEYING

Disturb not the ancient property line which thine ancestors established.

~Proverbs 22:28

I lifted up mine eyes again, and looked, and behold a man with a measuring line in his hand.

~Zechariah 2:1

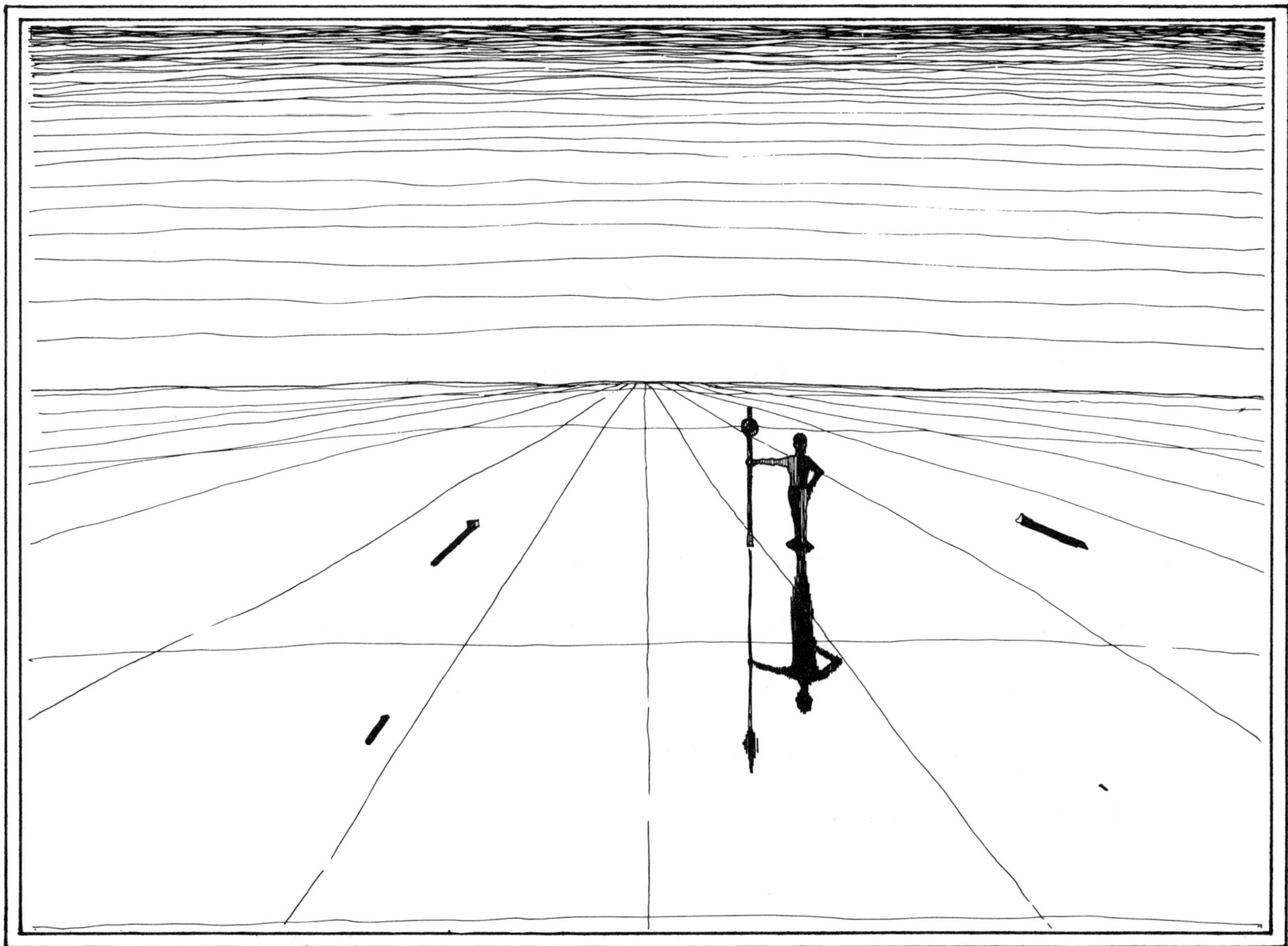

ON SITE PLANNING

Six feet of land was all that he needed.

~Leo Tolstoy (1886)

They are satisfied with their present lot and environment, and therefor do not want to conquer nature but merely be at home with nature and at peace with their lot.

~Hu Shih (1891~1962)

SIX
FEET
OF
LAND
WAS
ALL
HE
NEEDED

ON BUILDING PERMITS AND INSPECTIONS

It was built against the will of the Immortal Gods, and so it did not last for long.

~Homer: *The Illiad*, Book XII

Except the Lord build the house, they labor in vain that build it; except the Lord keepeth the city, the watchman walketh but in vain.

~Psalms 127:1

ON MATERIALS SELECTION

And they said one to another, Go to, Let us make brick, and burn them thoroughly. And they had brick for stone, and slime had they for mortar.

~Genesis 11:3

I found Rome a city of bricks and left it a city of marble.

~Augustus Caesar

The stone which the builders refused is become the headstone of the corner.

~Psalms 118:22; also Matthew 21:42

ON DESIGNING FOR THE HANDICAPPED

Thou shalt not ..... put a stumbling block before the blind.

~Leviticus 19:14

It seems more designed to make people stumble than to be walked upon.

~Franz Kafka : *The Great Wall of China, Reflections.*

CAUTION

ON TIME SCHEDULES

Rome was not built in one day.

~John Heywood (1497–1580)

But Solomon was building his own house

thirteen years, and he finished all his house.

~I Kings 7:1

AD
INFINITUM

ON BUDGETS AND WHERE THE MONEY GOES

Unto carpenters, and builders, and masons, and to buy timber and hew stone to repair the house.

~II Kings 22:6

And they gave the money, being told, into the hands of them that did the work, that had the oversight of the house of the Lord: and they laid it out to the carpenters and builders that wrought upon the house of the Lord.

~ II Kings 12:11

Nothing can be created from nothing.

~Lucretius: *De Rera Naturam*

For which of you, intending to build a tower,
sitteth not down first, and counteth
the cost, whether he hath sufficient to finish it?
Lest haply, after he hath laid the foundation,
and is not able to finish it, all that behold it
begin to mock him.

~St Luke 14:28-29

ON OVERZEALOUS DECORATORS

Now get you to my lady's chamber, and tell her, let her paint an inch thick.

~William Shakespeare: *Hamlet, act V, Scene I*

ON MAKING REVISIONS

It is a bad plan that admits of no modification.

~Publilius Syrus (1st. cen. B.C.)

ON CONVERTING TO METRIC

For it is not meters, but a meter-making argument that makes a poem -- a thought so passionate and alive that like the spirit of a plant or an animal it has an architecture of its own, and adorns nature with a new thing.

~Ralph Waldo Emerson: *Essays, Second Series* (1844)

ON DEMOLITION CONTRACTORS

Let me pry loose old walls. Let me lift and loosen old foundations.

~Carl Sandburg: *Prayers of Steel* (1920)

Herostratus lives that burnt the temple of Diana -- He is almost lost that built it.

~Sir Thomas Browne: *Urn-Burial or Hydiotaphia*.

ON OTHER SUBCONTRACTORS

Moreover there are workmen with thee in abundance, hewers and workers of stone and timber, and all manner of cunning men for every manner of work.
~I Chronicles 22:15

The carpenter stretcheth out his rule; he marketh it out with a line; he fitteth it out with planes, and he marketh it out with the compass.
~Isaiah 45:13

ON FOUNDATIONS

The house fell not: for it was founded on a rock.

~Matthew 7:25

As a wise master builder, I have laid the foundation and another buildeth upon. But let every man take heed how he buildeth upon.

~I Corinthians 3:10

ON HARDWARE

And David prepared iron in abundance for the nails for the doors of the gates, and for the joinings.

~I Chronicles 22:3

ON BUILDING A GOOD FIREPLACE

Sir, he made a chimney in my father's house, and the bricks are alive at this day to testify it.

~William Shakespeare: *Henry VI, Part II, act IV, Scene 2*

ON WALLS AND FENCES

He surveyed the fence, and all gladness left him and a deep melancholy settled down upon his spirit. Thirty yards of board fence nine feet high. Life to him seemed hollow and existence but a burden.

~Mark Twain: *The Adventures of Tom Sawyer*

Something there is that doesn't like a wall.

~Robert Frost

Don't ever take a fence down until you know the reason why it was put up.

~Ascribed to G.K. Chesterton by John F. Kennedy in a 1945 notebook.

Before I built a wall I'd ask to know what I was walling in or out.

~Robert Frost : *Mending Wall* (1914)

ON RELIGIOUS ARCHITECTURE

What is a church? Our honest sexton tells,
'Tis a tall building, with a tower and bells.

~ George Crabbe : *The Borough* (1810)

ON LEAVING INSTRUCTIONS WITH A SECRETARY

If anybody calls,
Say I am designing St. Paul's.
~Edmund Clerihew Bentley (1875-1956)

THE ARCHITECT'S
VADEMECUM
A. ALPERN
P. KRAEMER